Our Thang

Several Poems,
Several Drawings

OUR THANG
Several Poems, Several Drawings

POEMS
BY TED JOANS

DRAWINGS
BY LAURA CORSIGLIA

Ekstasis  Editions

National Cataloguing in Publication Data

Joans, Ted
Corsiglia, Laura
Our thang: selected poems, selected drawings

ISBN 1-894800-00-1

Poems. I. Title
PS8555.A7618R8413 2001   C843'.54   C00-911394-0
PR3919.2.C234R8413 2001

Published in 2001 by:
Ekstasis Editions Canada Ltd.
Box 8474, Main Postal Outlet   Box 571
Victoria, B.C. v8w 3s1   Banff, Alberta tol oco

Our Thang: Selected Poems, Selected Drawings has been published with
the assistance of a grant from the Canada Council for the Arts and the
British Columbia Arts Board, with the assistance of the Cultural Services
Branch of British Columbia
Printed in Canada

This book of drawings and poems is dedicated to
Marie Wilson and Charles Henri Ford

Contents

Introduction to the Drawings

The phrase "*Spirit of an Age*" conjures up a kind of synthesis of being right in a certain place at a certain time. Being of that time. Like most artists Laura is not of this time, nor of this place. Her residence is transience, and though a watcher of what is now, she is not consumed by it; rather she dances in and through it, much like her drawings in this book.

Looking at Laura's drawings spread out before me, the clear ideas of transformation and metamorphosis lead the viewer from one drawing to the next, but it is the notion of the Dance, and its rhythms (of revealing and concealing) in the individual drawings, and in the drawings as viewed sequentially that capture the imagination, and charge the drawings with potency.

In another time, I remember a glimpse I had of an old photograph of Laura as a young child standing amongst the Nisgaa in the presence of a recently killed very large grizzly bear. The great spirits move amongst us, looking for habitation, often find it in the heart of an artist. These highly anima(ted) drawings are evidence that the great bear spirit has found a welcome residence.

Harry Stanbridge

Why Selected Poems As Autobiography?

the point... at which the lived experience of *poésie*
becomes transformed into cultural memory. Inevitably, there will be
fewer and fewer witnesses to contribute to — or in my case *contest*
—the ideas about the past.

> Black America
> > music
> > folklore
> Bohemia America
> > avante-garde art
> > Beat movement
> Surrealist american
> > Europe
> Black Americain Africa
> > long distant safaris

Summation:
Teducation in the Black American tradition is not simply a matter of
holding the memory sacred, that is to be understood, but it is the
continuing existence of the past in my present.

Ted Joans

All

Dear poem
How are you?
I am well and do hope this
finds you poem -- the same.
I love you poem. Do you
still love the truth?
Poem I write you
because you
are the
truth
and
nothing but
the truth
dear poem
pure poem
our poem

Edinburgh 17 71 May

Another Dawn Dance

Sea with whales watching a movie-star whale
Sail through the air in plein air
Seals have soared across seas
Being whimsically tossed before being belly whaled

Seats of baggy green corduroy three leg trousers
Sold as secondeds Salivating Flea Market on
Saturdays by generous Will Flea Good
Brazen objective chance of objet-trouvés

Eat with silent silver sun on grown green eyes
Smiles never swallowed while dining
Shifts the cluttered canvas to tranquil blackground whisper
Drawn brown hirsute grey graphic l'amour fou man

At another dawn when desire invites the dance
Sauntering bed sheets with passion black berries jamming
Strut horizontal while licking canyon wall-bearings
Rear rhino rapture mirror remains toujours pour la premiere fois

Seattle hard handful of empty skyscrapers
Seething with inner city envy to digest their steepness
Rising horizon of kneaded cloudick saluted at dawn
Bear licked lascivious under T-shirt tout de suite

Supernest breast displayed above fried monte carlo manuscript
Sensual plastic wall spread readied for uptight action
Toiletissue sandwiched to raw canvas' needed thighs
Rubber whale swims in aged sperm joy juice le vin nouveau

Another dawn dance near by wrists of crows and gulls
Illuminated rain roof reflect riceless high priced paddies
Draperies await rejuvenated finger tongue gestures
Languishing lengthy head hair hiccups bold bald top's danse d'aube encore
        10 January 1996

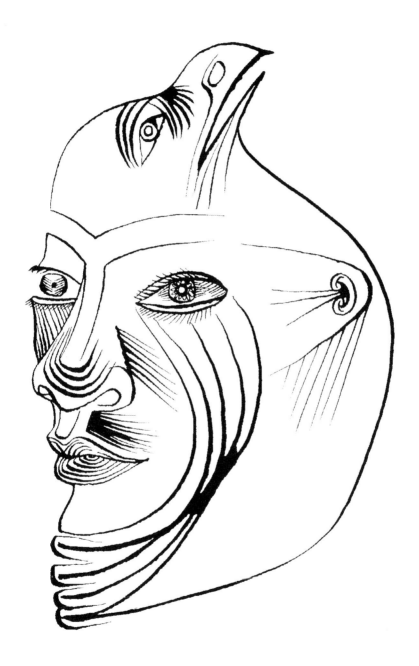

Laura Corsiglia 1999

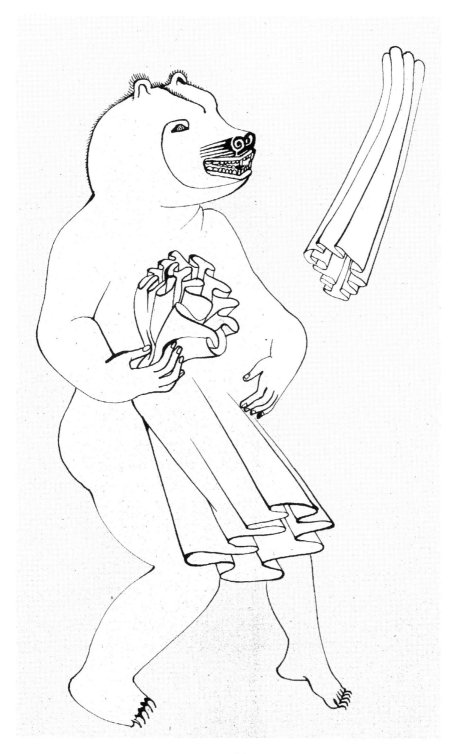

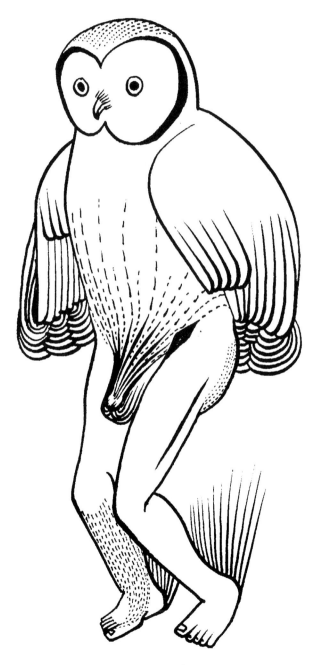

B before B

The alphabet B
Is infesting my brain
Brain starts with b
B is before me
Like rain follows b
Like Ain in Algeria
Those ain this
Ain that in Morocco
Tunisia – perhaps
Paul Bowles is
Hip to other ains
B as in Bowles
Contaminates me
B is brain beginning
Rain follows b
Ain follows b
In follows b
Brion Gysin is hip
To Ains
He too has suffered
Saharan surprises that
B played major role
B as in Berber brain
B as in burnoose
B as in balek balek
B as in the bab door
The letter b
Ignites into creative
Beings such as
Basquiat
Bearden
Breton

Bird
Clifford Brown
Benjamin Péret
Bill Traylor
Amiri Baraka
Frédéric Bruly Bouabré
He be a Bété poete
He like Baraka be
Still here with us
Unlike other V.I.P. B
For excellent example
B as Buddy Bolden
B as Bessie Smith
And even b in
Bix Beiderbecke
Bunny Berigan too
B as the ultimate:
Mr. B the Billy Eckstine
B of brilliant Bebop
And my Apple teachers
Babs Gonzales
Bob Reisner
These two never got to the
Bambara
Bamileke
Bobo Bozo or Bakuba
Fortunately they indirectly
Helped my preparation
Babs and Bob
Trumpet I attempted
To blow
As all musicians know
Are in cozy key of B-flat
I tried imitating John B.
B stands for Birks
John Birks Dizzy Gillespie

So in a short trumpet
Tooting time
I stopped beeping
When I should have bopped
Dizz's technique caused
Me to stop professionally
It is always for me black blues
To be or not to bop
And there is always Mr.B.
That all important "B"
Bicornis the endangered
African rhinoceros
Popular called
Black rhino due to its
Power and its
Black humor
Brooklyn botanical and
Zoological Garden is where
Black rhino bicornis
I first did see 1951
Alive and recognizable
Both bicornis horns intact
Piano Bud is wiser
Than the black general all know
Big crash of rhinoceroses
I dug before I was
Bigger than the Apple
That I was to come to
Bursting out of
Birth placenta balloon
Blossoming under-rated
By best-minds of
Beat Generation
B is still the magnet
B sound
B as in Betye

First one befriended
Yes "befriend", be friend me
Placed me in sacred Harlem pad
Blond bricks Strivers Row
Black power apartment
Betye the first
Placed me for few days
In His Hipness' OAAU H.Q.
Brother Malcolm X's pad
Alone I few night-day there
Spirits that enhance
Instructed my directions
During the quiet apartment
Black nights in Harlem
Better Crust Pie bakery
Be doing soul potato
Sweet blessed pie business
What Malcolm X ghost said
"If you don't know– learn
If you already know – teach!"
He left the world these keys
Brilliant or shadowy poemlife
One as I don't care to please
Betye the second
She be real
Million times more real
Than her Hollywood backdrop
B for bold poetic objects
B for Betye Saar
The beauty Saar artist
Convulsive sorceress she
Who carries her eggs to
Where they hatch baskets
Bridge baskets unscrambled
Beautiful cutiful Betye
B the alphabet I bet

B as in Beauford
Beauford Delaney
Brother to Joseph
Both painters
Beauford known
Brother unknown
Both long gone to ancestors
Beauford of yesteryear bohemia
Beauford of Paris paint scene
Beauford last seen in asylum
Beauford who could dance
Beauford another Afro
Important B of nouveau
Beaux-art worthiness
Bambaras of the Bronx
Bakuba of Brooklyn
Hausa Hebrew influenced
Taking Care Bizness T.C.B.
Baltimore to Benin City
Berlin to Bobodioulasso
And me myself & I
Teducating in ole Buktu
The sacred letter B
Has infested me
Eventhough there's
No "b" in any of my names
In any of my totem
Mammal animal names
Nor is there a question as
To be or not
To be a "b"
Beset or dissect "B"
You'll get a number
Thirteen -a "1" a "3"
Nevertheless
I be (unlike yall!)

I Be natural in music b
I Bewitched in sorcery
I Besmirch the few enemies
By belittling their worthiness
Bespatter them with frozen
Benign neglect of their
Worldly invisiblism
Besides I be blatantly
Their numero uno
Bête noire
Bestir me not!
I the anvil bezal
I bewilder so beware
I refuse to bemoan
Such an insignificant bevy
Nevertheless
Who touched my hand
Betwixt bicentennial of
Butter of better peanuts
Beserk edification crime
Stars that reflect only
Sun as I son of the sun
B still burns in/out me
Ask the cast of thousand
Better yet, demand the casts
Of thirty thousand
Baobab that I be
A ten branch tree almost
As many as great Dame
La Baker Josephine
Not as great writer
Baldwin, Jimmy James
Not as great nightimer
Late Hart Leroy Bibbs was
He who Double-Trouble
Made be

I be decades ago
Bestowed upon by
Brown, Sterling the poet
He who said
"You (be) are the
Personification of this poem
"Long Gone"
"I don't know which way
I'm travelin'–
Far or near, All I know
fo' certain is
I cain't stay here."
That poem be
Exactly me
Bulawayo is the
Big B town of Bulova
Watch watching clock tick
Country of Zimbabwe
But Botswana is
Gonna be
A next visit to
Kalahari Desert
Femmoiselle and me
Borough of Manhattan
Behoove such an island
But Lamu
Boost such awesome too
Bowels move
Allowing intestine vacancy
A moveable feces
Smell odor stronger but
Butt no longer
Hemmed in sphincter way
Bowel boulevards open
Anal avenues way free
Flowing water flames

Big rootie tootie blast
Boisterous Saturday mail
Bulges threateningly from
Box that post persons
Genuflect and gesture
They being carrier-pigeons
Entrusted with officialdom
Bring proposition to do
Or not-to-do
What other major publishers
Should-would-could
Have done done
Place on the shelves
Public and private shelves
Perhaps a single volume
Better still a larger
Book of known and
Unknown poems
By me myself & I
Dedicated to two worthy
Blacks of modern world
One known
One unknown
Reflecting the poems
Published upon these pages
Boat dinner ride
Bay of Elliott (Puget Sound)
Bowels breed bad manners
Bus rides to exhibit
Boostering artist with words
Best show upward to go
Boat first dance done did
Late night trolley home
Bought our big bread cost
Air tickets to the Apple
Bob Thompson retro-late respect

Done did then
Off to Paris exhibit
Basquiat gallerie show
But Timbuktu priority
Blasting bold words in
Teducate tribute to
Brother Basquiat
Had visual focused dream
Breton at a desk
Behold a crystal gift
I presented it to him
After unwrapping it
He was pleased
Expressed how marvelous
This old antique was
Now that had been
Transformed from its
Original foundation and function
I toiled all night until 5:45 AM
After writing the largest
Personal check I had ever
Twice as much as
Wesley lit agentry check
He who expressed mail
Photos and Ferlinghetti news
To our eyes this
Early autumn day
Having paid two months
Advance rent in checks
Now must do same for
Communcations US West
We wear our shorts
We still short sleeve
Safari jackets but soon
We must switch to warmer and longer
Sleeves and trouscrs

Having phoned Magali
La fashion modelextraordinaire
Requesting a stay
In her spacious pad
No response as yet
It is almost like
Playing a game of cards
In the game of staying
A few days
In that city
In their pad
At this time
Play an ace
And one has a place
Even with unlimited
Entry and exit
Play a king or queen
Not too good unless
You share a late late
Night social scenes
We be worn out
After all museums
We all day visit
The game goes on
Play the cards
Straight from the deck
Remain cautious
One does not know
What is next
Unless host is happy
Not at all depressed
Still yet there could be
Surprisingly a severe
Case of urban stress
That is the joker
In the card game

Of staying
Friends-acquaintances
And strangers
P.B. are two
United Staters of
Long-time dwelling
In Africa
On cuntinent places
P.B. numéro uno is
Paul Bowles
P.B. nummer zwei is
Peter Beard
Both bold brave men
Have wandered around
Their chosen
African geographic grounds
P.B. #1 in North Africa
P.B. #2 in East Africa
Both are aqcuaintances of
Allover Africa —— me
Being there is better
You'd better
Believe it be!

18 September 1998

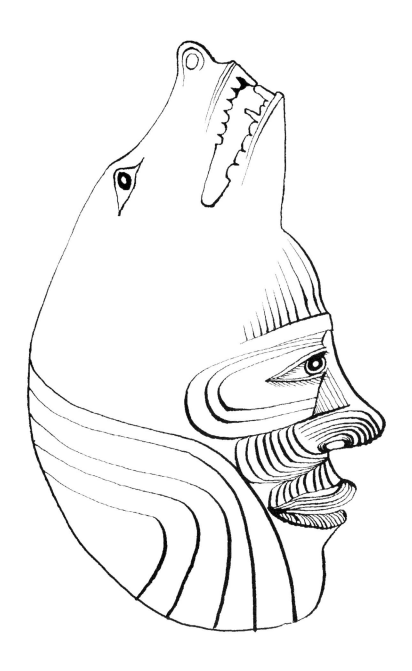

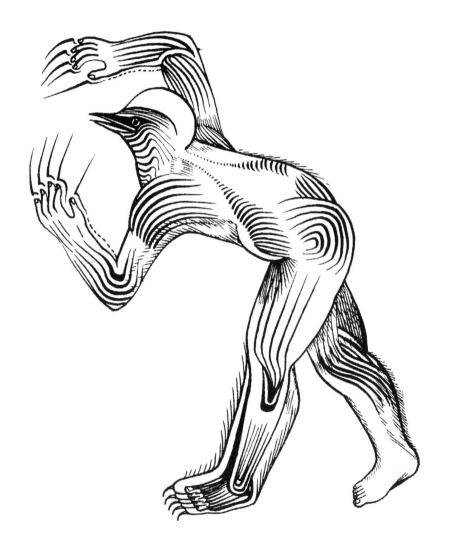

Laura Corsiglia 1999

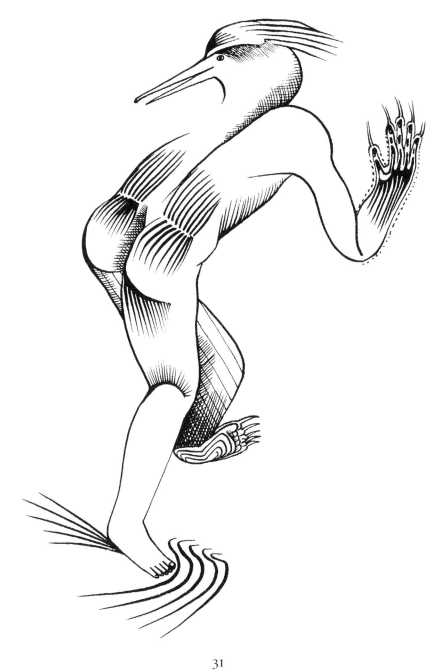

Dream Undreamt

for Laura

Je l'entends comme
Je me vois.
Oui, mes amies comme
As I see myself
Je me vois
Under a full moon
After teducating
A crowded crunch of
Men who'd heard
During cherry tree
Urban blossoming time
Burnt Church
Medicine Hat
Yellow Knife
What poems await
In those concealed
Canadian places
When shall they
Become world renown
Comme Je Me Vois
In C.A.A.S. book form
Or another
Fred Macfoto Beat
His Herstory book
Burnt Church
Medicine Hat
Yellow Knife
Dwellers snore there
No golfers grow there
Tigers of yellow stripes
On black championship bodies
Do not roam woods

Bare headed
Medicine mad hat woman
Which burnt church ruins
Conceals perfidious pages
Of How To Live Longer
But not be stronger
Comme je me vois
As hot crows nest sun
First day then
Second half day of hail
Weather wanders B.C.
Long before Christ
Why not apply A.G.
Allen the Ginsberg one
Who maybe hero
In Yellow Knife
His howling bardic beard
Dust has sharpened
Youth of Yellow Knife
Why not rhinoceroses
Race tracked
During summertime
Burnt Church
No rhinos carry
Mad cow bad mouth disease
Speculate such mumbling
Comme je me vois
As rhino trainer
As jockey
Also rhino racer winner
Only seven species
Unlike anvils
Only Asian and African rhinos
No European rhinoceros
Although one is hip
To anvil facts of Europe

Comme je me vois
Wood balsam anvil smooth
Styrofoam giant anvil rough
Cuddly cotton stuff anvil
Manufactured like matchsticks
In Yellow Knife
In Medicine Hat
In Burnt Church
Visionary painters live there
Some suggest being
Adolf Wölfli late period
Bill Traylor early offerings
Henri le douanier Rousseau
Upon retirement
No traffic jams or jellies
Nor penis buttered
In those places
Where rhino race tracks
Remain round
Perfected circles
One quarter mile length
Ten meters wide
Electronic clay track
Loud broadcast of
Rapid running rhinos
More faster than
Human gloved toes
He mail@She mail.com there
Faxophone too
Risks have been
Run out of town!
Ask plenty bodies
Citizens of
Yellow Knife they know
Medicine Hat they know
Burnt Church chicks & cats

Age eight to eighty
Have always
Been hip to such facts
Sip quiet cognacs
At their tourniquet of
Lamu sundowners
Bite edible scissor handles
At the wine soaked diapers
Of Timbuctoo rough roof erotics
Break water and wind
During daily stroll
Along the bird beaches
As tired working women
Walk their housetrained
Husbands on leashes
Sunsetters witness this
Tallest pole salutes it
A gorgeous group
On uniformed trees
Sing in almost silent tongues
Soft shoe rhino lover
Hugs a smiling ornithologist
She his freemale amie
Today vogelforscher
Demain back to bears
Furfeather lady of flowers
I hear her as a song
Comme je me vois

9 April 2001

Laura Corsiglia
1999

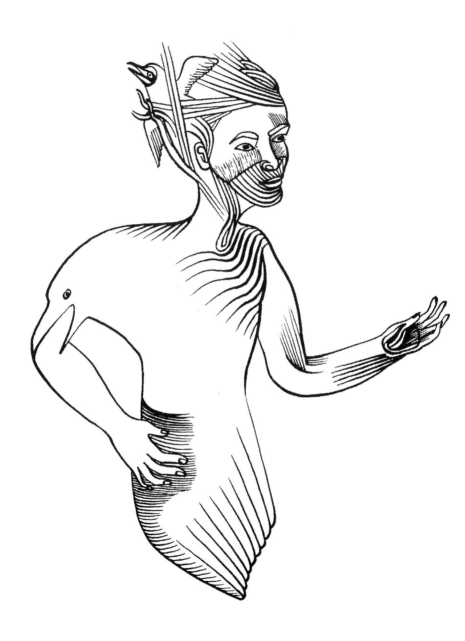

I've Got Your Haha, Heehee & Ho Ho

What ever you've lost
I, Found IT!
Wherever you lost it
I found it Yes, you heard correct
I found it !
What you lost
When you lost it
Wherever you lost it
It was I who found it
Do you still remember
What it was you lost?
Did you search for it ?
When you discovered
That you had lost it?
How you lost it
Why you lost it
What time you lost it

Never Mind !
Best to forget it !
I FOUND IT ! !
It was your lost bag
It contained your personal
This and thats
It was important to you
It was so very very important to you!
It was all lost in your bag
Losing it makes you sad
And even mad!
Because all was lost
Never you mind !
Best to forget it

I found it
Yes,it is true I'm telling you
That I found it !
It was your special thing
It was perhaps your engagement or wedding ring
It was surely valuable
It was maybe an irreplaceable gift
It was one of a kind
STOP LOOKING FOR IT !!
Cause you'll not ever find
For it was that !
I found it

WASN'T IT your set of keys ?
WASN'T IT your fatass backpocket billfold ?
WASN'T IT your wonderful expensive watch ?
WASN'T IT your special trusty writing pen ?
WASN'T IT your borrowed diamond bracelet or necklace?
If that is the case
Best to forget it yes you are correct
I found it !!

WASN'T IT that scarf, hat, glove, cap, umbrella, bicycle, coat, wheel-
chair, shoulder bag, top coat, suitcase, sunglasses,monkey wrench,
shoe shine kit, note book, anvil, can of caviar, cosmetic compact,
address book, bank book, cook book, tool box, ice tongs, shower
rungs, clarinet, false teeth, walking cane, sewing kit, unloaded
revolver, one bow and seven arrows, an artificial
eyeball, an inscribed Talmud Torah, a talking portable Bible, a rare
antique Koran, a left hand shaving kit, a trumpet mouth piece, a cas-
sette recorder, a video cassette, an awful costly camera, a portable
toilet, a lightweight guide book of the world, an accordion of credit
cards, a French accordion in the key of MONK (Thelonius, that is!),
a bottle of Champagne, a large jar of peanutbutter, a brand new pair
of sneakers, a plastic bag of health food groceries, a small but vicious
dog, a large lazy black teddy bear's wind up key, a pair of twin eyed

binoculars, a wheelbarrow, a faded blue comb, a childhoodlunchbox,
a hard hat, A PIGGY BANK, A DIPLOMATIC POUCH CONTAIN-
ING ILLEGAL THIS AND OF COURSE THATS!! a sewing machine,
a portable dissecting table, an erotic umbrella made of sponges, ten-
nis racket, aluminium cigar case, a pool table, a portable swimming
pool, a luggage rack, a baseball mit,a baseball glove,an unbearble base
ball fulla autographs, a pocket watch, a wrist watch,a miniature watch
tower, a monogram silver lighter, a folding bed, a folding desk, a
toothpick of silver, an Old Master painting, a first edition and
inscribed to you, a birth certificate, a passport with your personal
expiration date officially on it, and
there was that precious something that nobody knew of but you, you
lost that along with all those other mentionables, and you also lost
your private unmentionables along with your ticket, your computor
card and a stack of
crisp U.S.Godollar one hundred bills...!!!
Best to relax and just forget it
Because you have
Yes you have
Actually lost it
And
I found it !

21 June 1993 Den Haag Holland

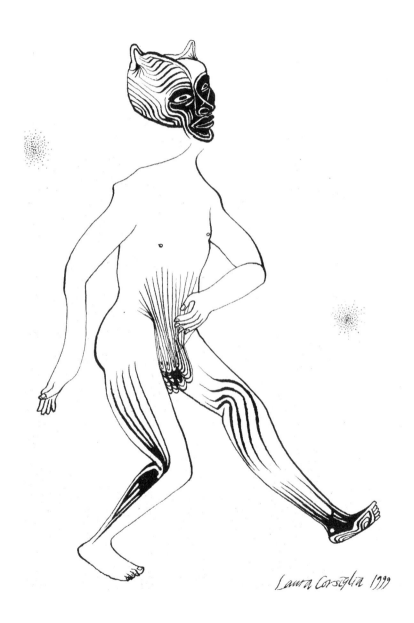

Laura Corsiglia 1999

Laura Corsiglia 1999

44

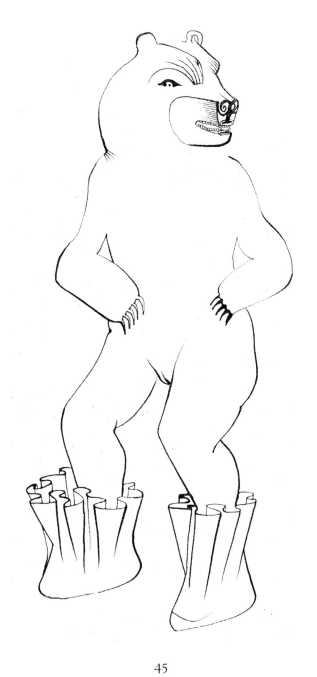

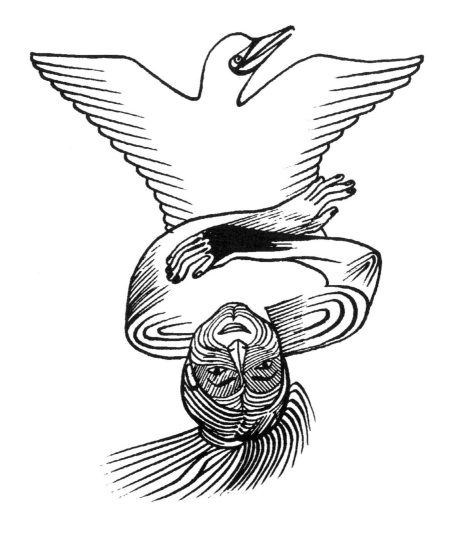

Laura Corsiglia 2000

47

NO COACHING

No Coaching Please
Please out of respect
Go a way
Or stand back
Way way back
When I begin
To pack

Please dont ask
To see this
Item or
That thing there
While I'm
Trying to pack

Best for you
To leave me alone
Let me be
In full charge
Of my packing

I'm self packing
My bags
My trunk
My suitcases
So please
Do not meddle
With my valise

Dont stand around
I am leaving
As soon as
I'm packed

Yes leaving town
Please dont muddle
My packing up mind

Stop asking me
Who & what & why
Which & where & when
Or how I am
Going to 'make a
LIVING' again!

Please let me be
Respect my method
Of packing these
Things that
Belong solely to me

I do not want
To hear your
Opinion about
How you would pack
Breakable items
My judgement
Is my packing way

Go a way
Go sit down
Scram outta sight
Read a travel book
Just please
Do me a great favor
By allowing me
To P A   C K
Peacefully

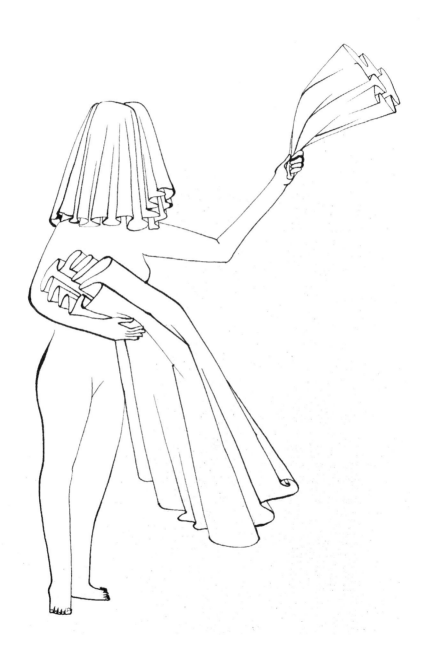

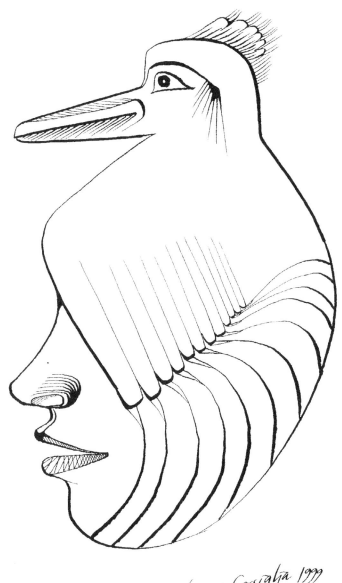

Laura Casiglia 1999

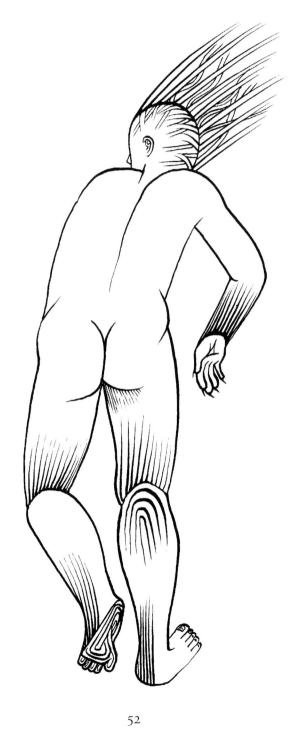

NOT ON MOST MAPS

It is written
It is said
That this precious
Place on special maps
Is actually
The Tombouctou de France

It is visited
In certain seasons
By selective persons
Who repetitively come
Here (this lofty village)
For highly personal reasons

It is upper cliff sides
It is down southwest wise
Almost the naval of dreams
But one can conventionally conjure
Multi-view postcard yet
Unique as Mali's Timbuktu

It is not
At all well known
That this magic spot
Has an alchemy of its own
That welcomes one
Without murmuring a word

It too like Paris
Is feminine town
Although no pollution make-up
That erodes its marvelous beauty
This fresh body of Vieux France
A living surreality-named
St-Cirq-Lapopie

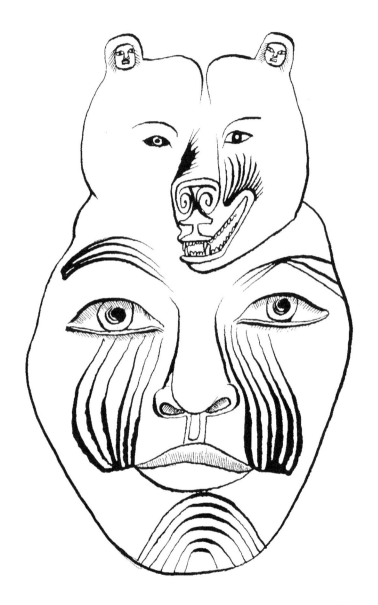

Laura Corsiglia 1999

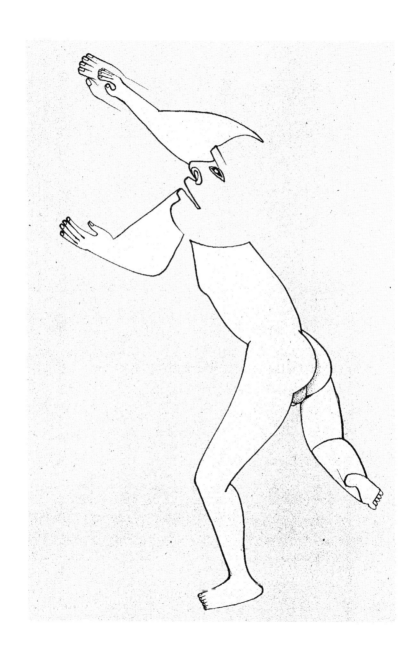

55

NEW HOODOO ON YOU KNOW WHO

WHO DO
YOU DO
HARMFUL
HATEFUL
HORRIFIC
HYSTERIC HOODOO
          ON
THEIR BEST BIRTHDAY
THEIR WISE WEDDING DAY
THEIR HILARIOUS HAPPY HOLIDAY
         WHO DO DAT?
YOU   WHO DONE DID
VOODOO
LONG DISTANTLY
        SO WELL
NOW WILL YOU
H O O D O O
V O O D O O
IF THEY WEAR GRIGRI
OR JUJU
AND THEY MOJO
BE WORKING OVERTIME ?

12 NOV 1983 BERLIN

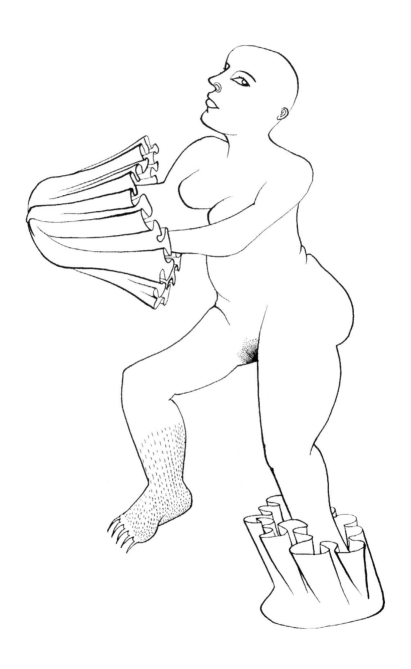

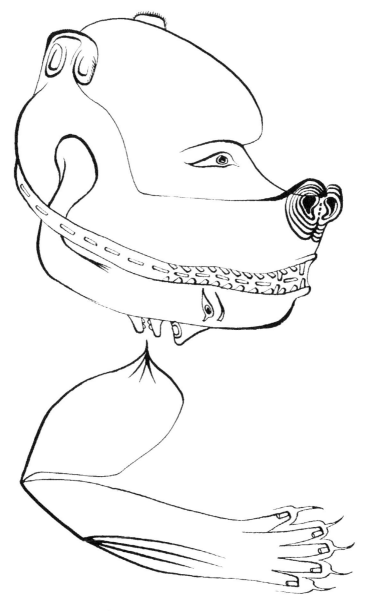

Laura Corsiglia   2000

59

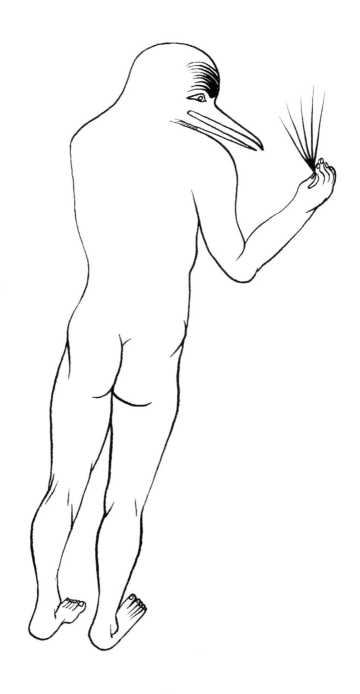

The Dreaded S.A.S.E.

He was the personification
Of the original Beat scener
On the outside
With self pride
Never caring to be
Inside of any scene
His scene was unique
Brave to remain Beat
Reading poems his poetry
On crowded
And uncrowded streets
The slender Micheline man
Stretching from New York
To San Francisco
If Ginsberg was Guernica
And Corso was Uccello's
Battle of Romano
And Ferlinghetti was
Walt Disney's Donald Duck
Then Jack Micheline was
Goya's Disasters of War
He was limited edition
Of superb etchings
A rare steel engraving
Jack who wore the French
Double rubber tyre name
Jack who was honored
To have Jack the Kerouac one
Introduce his first verse
They both enjoyed bathing
In rivers of red wine
Micheline was a great
Great gift and gifted
A wonderful gift
Of self inflicted carelessness

His own carelessness
Spilled out spontaneously
Amongst the needy
Micheline a no-nonesense man
Designed by hard dues
He was hip to the
Art of celebration

Never heeding to
Dreaded S.A.S.E.
Not Jack Micheline !
For he was a natural
Self Adressed Poet
Stamped Enveloped Poet
To the big publishers
Who automatic demand
The dreaded S.A.S.E.
Jack's spirit prevails
Amongst you worthy poet ones
And you too who are
The "wannabe" and
Also (far too many) "wannaBeats"
Yes you & you & you
Those S.A.S.E. postal poets

Feb 32 1998 Seattle Wash

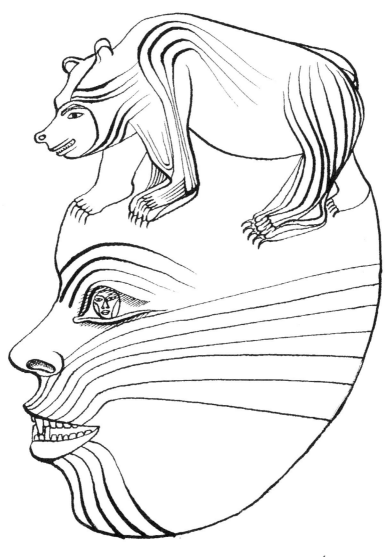

Laura Corsiglia 1999

63

Laura Corsiglia 1999

64

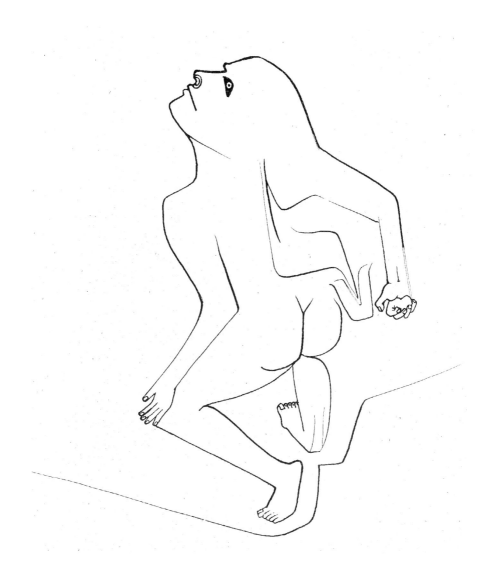

WHO SHOOK

IT WAS ONLY YESTERDAY
THAT I DEFENDED
A WHITE
RHINOCEROS
AND HAVING DONE SO
THE TWO NAUGHTY
FRENCH BOY SCOUTS
RAN AWAY
THE RHINOCEROS
FELT RELIEVED
IT CAME OVER
NEAR ME
AND STOOD
I REACHED OVER
THE WALL
TO RUB ITS
DUSTY HARD BACK
THE HAND THAT I
RUBBED THIS GREAT
LAND MAMMAL
HAD SHOOKED
the hand of André Breton
who had shook
the hand of Apollinaire
who had shook
the hand of Picasso
who had shook
the hand of Wifredo Lam
who had shook
the hand of Nicolas Guillén
who had shook
the hand of Langston Hughes
who had shook

the hand of Léon Damas
who had shook
the hand of Aimé Césaire
who had shook
the hand of Malcolm X
who had shook
the hand of Dick Gregory
who had shook
the hand of Steve Allen
who had shook
the hand of Jack Kerouac
who had shook
the hand of Allen Ginsberg
who had shook
the hand of Leroi Jones
who had shook
the hand of John Coltrane
who had shook
The hand of Albert Ayler
who had shook
the hand of Cecil Taylor
who had shook
the hand of Ornette Coleman
who had shook
the hand of Jayne Cortez
who had shook
the hand of Don L.Lee
who had shook
the hand of Gwendolyn Brooks
who had shook
the hand of Hoyt Fuller
who had shook
the hand of Stokley Carmicheal
who had shook
the hand of Kwame Nkrumah
who had shook

the hand of Lumumba
who had shook
the hand of Louis Armstrong
who had shook
the hand of Duke Ellington
who had shook
the hand of Billie Holiday
who had shook
the hand of Thelonious Monk
who had shook
the hand of Charlie Parker
who had shook
the hand of Bud Powell
who had shook
the hand of Max Roach
who had shook
the hand of Lionel Hampton
who had shook
the hand of Betty Carter
who had shook
the hand of Dizzy Gillespie
who had shook
the hand of Charlie Mingus
who had shook
the hand of Kenneth Patchen
 who had shook
the hand of Richard Wright
who had shook
the hand of James Baldwin
who had shook
the hand of Beauford Delaney
who had shook
the hand of Jacob Lawrence
who had shook
the hand of Romare Bearden
who had shook

the hand of Joan Miró
who had shook
the hand of Sidney Bechet
who had shook
the hand of Jean Paul Sartre
who had shook
the hand of Frantz Fanon
who had shook
the hand of Robert Goffin
who had shook
the hand of René Magritte
who had shook
the hand of Giorgio de Chirico
who had shook
the hand of Cogollo
who had shook
the hand of Matta
who had shook
the hand of Joyce Mansour
who had shook
the hand of Benjamin Péret
who had shook
the hand of Marie Wilson
who had shook
the hand of Frida Kahlo
who had shook
the hand of Manuel Bravo
who had shook
the hand of Octavio Paz
who had shook
the hand of Jean Clarence Lambert
who had shook
the hand of Luis Buñuel
who had shook
the hand of Robert Benayoun
who had shook

the hand of Konrad Klapheck
who had shook
the hand of Joseph Beuys
who had shook
the hand of Marcel Duchamp
who had shook
the hand of Charles Henri Ford
who had shook
the hand of Man Ray
who had shook
the hands of an electrician, a baker, a cobbler,
a long distance truck driver, a basket baller,
plain plane pilot, chef, janitor, concierge, waiter,
brick layer, tree surgeon, doctor, grocer, mechanic,
farmer, plumber, tailor, dentist, librarian, acrobat,
garbage man, post person, a merchant seaman
who was in charge of the ship
that brought from Africa safely
one white rhinoceros
to the Paris Zoo
TO BE LOOKED AT
AND PROTECTED
FROM ME AND YOU

7 JUIN 1985

Laura Cosigna 1999

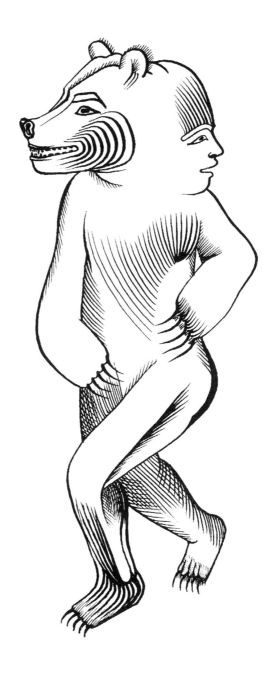

72

Wood Works

in memory of Peter Wood

Born as a living
Tower of Pisa
Where its velvet stairs
Conceal only the best
Wines that are blessed
By Benjamin Peret
A machine eats only
Guns manufactured by
Prag gypsies whom are
Wellknown cotton &
Pocket pickers
Woods of leaves that dont come back
Thick baobabs around
These luney leaning towers
Fullmoon flashes warnings
"If life matters, so do hours"
This menu mention causes
Tower of Pizza, Tower of Pity
and Tower of Pisa to
Take the voluptous shape of
Hourglass , therefore
insuring each empty
Glass eye to be filled
Each hour by oar
Own waiter no
Matta whats the Matta
The work had been done!
Terminal made of wood
Guards hired by pangolins
Who serve gloves with
Seven thumbs on
Every bomb day

Prohibited in or outside
The non-leaning tower
Stuffed with syrups
More bitter than
Hitler's defeat
Stalin's cold feet
Old Victoria Queen's
Con game imperial seat
Crosseyed vomits her
Smoke erupts from
Towers ears that
Escalate around towersides
An orange eats an apple
In grape shadow it
Is worked asthough
Benin brass in wood
A wonder thunder of
Wood work
Termites proved the
Tower's fact whilst
Realms of mosquito
Known in Bali he was
To sweat blood
Staining packs of wet
Cigarettes with rats
Sharp cruxifix used to
Stab undead steaks that
Sun themselves well done indeed!
The bent tower who
Became bent from too-much
Unwanted oats and fame on beer
Helping cartons of books to escape
From Rue de la Montagne Sainte Genevieve
And from Rue Larrey where once
Duchamp had adored an
Open-closed door nearby

A mist mosque served Friday
Only wood work
Out of the Bois into
Delhi pyre fire
Infested forests of ever & nevergreens
 that glove like glows
that grows against such
Official grain with
Clean neck tie in which
The knot is open bottle
Inwhich a sinking ship
Refuses to drown in
The shape of super sip lips
That alert lovers that
Eat & sleep crenelates holy
Wood accented by splintery
Planks as stone would have half done

4/7/99

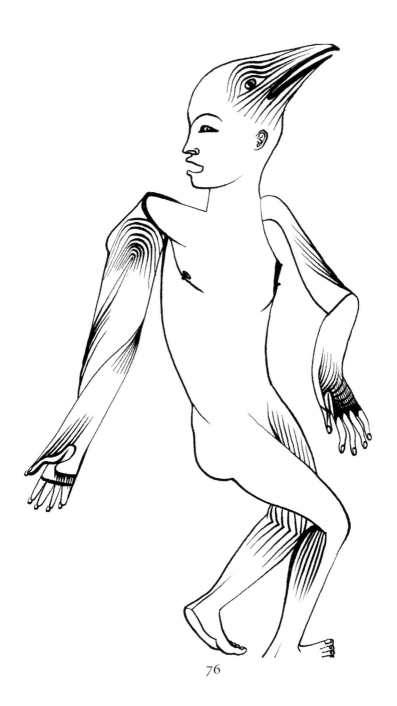

YES YOU HAVE !

Yes you have
You may not admit it
You perhaps do not care
for it to be known
But Oh yes you have!
 Yes Oh yes you have
Gone to bed
Undressed
Bare
Naked
Y e s
Nude
Gone to bed with
a mosquito !

Yes you have
Oh yes you have
Gone to bed
without any clothes on
with a mosquito

Yes you have
Remember how it
sung to you
as it circled
over your
bare body
Oh yes it was
NAKED YOU !

Remember it waited
Watched your nudity
as it happidly sung

Remember when
you went to sleep
It was then
that mosquito stung

Yes you have
slept with
a mosquito
Yes it was you
who slept naked
Undressed
Bare body
Unashamed
Yes it is true
You went to bed
with a mosquito!

Oakland 21 April 1985

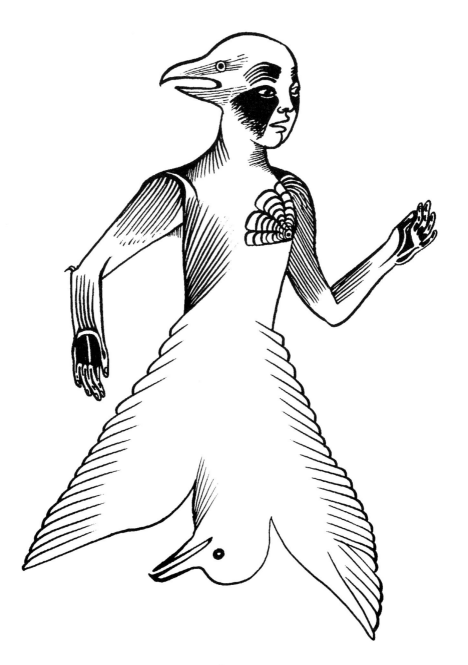

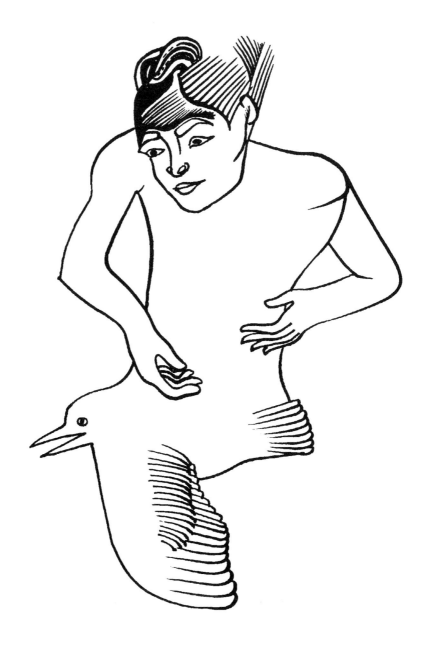

Ye Olde Hysteric Replay

Here after twenty years
Does he stand
In the same locale
In similar pose
Clad in much better clothing
Although the footwear
Is not black this time
But worn just the same
smudged white sneakers
He has grown a bushy
Salt and pepper beard
It has been two decades
Since he on this exact
correct date and corner
Stood defiant yet Beat
Just a few giant steps
From the Hotel Beat
At numero neuf
Rue Git-le-Coeur
Now Ye Olde Historic
Beat Hotel has gone
Yet he stands under
A new street sign
Where the old original
Paris street sign useta hang
He is doing a literary replay
of the yesteryears
Beat generated glory days
On Rue Git-le-Coeur
Where all hearts opened
And some thighs did too
When all wines flowed

There in Paris a target
Of on the road hipsters
This street where the
Truth lies

July 11, 1980 3:00 AM
waiting for the dawn to arrive

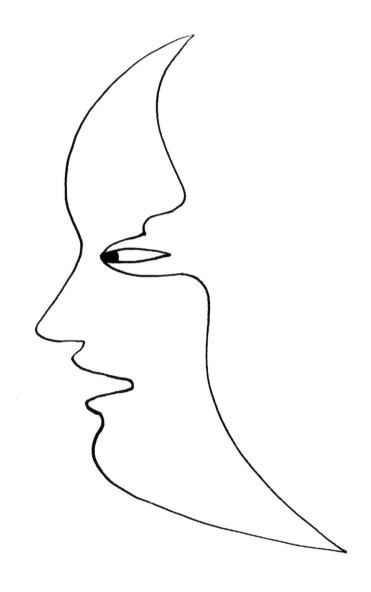

85

Quincaillerie

At the hardware (quincallerie) one can buy
And perhaps get high from the pot
One can buy in all shapes, fashion, and forms
At the quincaillerie (hardware) one can score
And maybe get higher more from a new pot
All the pot hanging on the walls
Big, medium, large, and shiny tiny pot on shelves
At the hardware stores (pot shop)
One can help themselves to pot pot pot
Plenty pot
Legally got
But late pot can be very hot
so be
cool when
you fool
with
pot!

Timimoun, Algerie Jan 4 75

S O N day Poem

for Russell K.J.

He rubbed his little brown nose
against mine
He took my big hand with
his small hand
and off we walked
across the world
wearing smiles
having fun
Me god
His father
He god
My son

His eyebrows are his
yet arched like his mother
Harlem is his natural look
although Scotland is stuck
on his polite tongue like tape
His energy endless and
interest insatiable   all true
However that makes my son
so wonderful to see
He is a new
Better version
Of me!

30 May 1971

Attention Taxi Drivers

Taxi Drivers should be nice
To strangers who sit behind them
Taxi drivers whom are evil or rude
Usually vanish where nobody can find them
Taxi drivers should be friendly
To passengers who pay with a smile
Taxi drivers whom are kind
Exist to old age and longer, while
Taxi drivers that act bad or mean
Often are found body separated from head
Or worst just dead
Never ever to be seen
London taxis/ Paris taxis/ Amsterdam taxis/
Hamburg taxis/ Accra taxis/ Lagos taxis
Please do read and take taxi heed

9/1/75

Dontcha Dare!

Dont make fun
Of my collard greens
My grits, pies, chitterlins,
And other foodstuff
Dont make fun
Of what I eat
Cause life for me
Has been so rough
Dont make fun
Of the way I walk
As I diddybop
Down the street
Dont make fun
Of my large, but reliable
Big powerful feet
Dont go laughing
At the way I laff
When my mouth
Is filled with mirth
And souls full of Joy
Dont go giggling
At my shout
In my own Sunday church
Dont signify me—boy

Dont make fun
Of the way I walk
Cause my tongue
Jes be that way
I done been
To school and back
Peoples unnerstan what
I and they say
Fortunately
My speech is Black

So dont poke derisively
At my naturalness:
They way I dance
They way we walk
What we eats
And the way we greets
And even our own
Black style of dressing

Just 'member
I'm just black natural
Our unique culture
Is our blessing
It teaches y'all a lesson!

Corona, Queens   13 Sept 75

41 Bullet Lynch

       Anvils had not caused the
       Uncrime death of
       Unabled semen to
       Spurt into Abel Tasman's
       Mother who
       Had never sodomized
       Thylacine marsupials
Uncle Thomas of Supreme
U.S. Courtship flinched
Forty one times as
Bullet patches cut through
His funky black robe
He knew no flow of
Guinean boubou robe
No Nimba Picasso influence
Still yet four NYPD
Pull trigger forty one
Lynch-all-male-nigger time
Fortunately for thylacine
It is not a dog
Not at all a canine
Its carnivorous taste
Is to eat victim's
Brains, liver that quiver
Kidneys that fail safe
Thylacine similar to four
NYPD Forty one Trigger Jerks
It washes all down
In fresh blood
Or beers with
Other police brothers
Anvils that fly
Swift shall splat
Four until forty one
Fortunately are revenged

Their badge's edges
Razor sharp to
Slice forty one official
NYPD eyeballs an
Intro to AfroAndalusian
Dog them til death
The four Caucasoid male
Beings who trigger-pulled
Forty one bullet-
Blasting into black
Body imported from
Africa times
Condemn them by
Any means necessary:
Stroll before their homes
Scrawl or stencil forty one
Near their frequented environs
Attend their houses of worship
Prey upon them psychological
Release forty one means
To each of the four to die
Abel Tasman suggest this

27 June 2000

Laura Corsiglia was raised in northern British Columbia's Nass Valley surrounded by grizzly bears. Her first art experiences were masks, dances, songs and totem poles of the Nisga'a indiginenous people for whom her parents worked. She later grew up in Victoria, BC, and now lives in Vancouver. Exten sive travelling and an education at Paris Ecole National Superieure des Beaux-Arts added an international element to her respect for Bears in all forms. Her work has been exhibited all over the world, from Paris to London to New York to Seattle. She came to surrealism through the arts of the Pacific Northwest Coast.

Ted Joans describes himself as a "Jazz poet, thus a revolutionary poet," a painter and a former trumpet player. Born in Cairo, Illinois, in 1928, of parents who worked an annual river-boat run on the Mississippi. His father, a riverboat entertainer, put him off the boat in Memphis at age twelve and gave him a trumpet. He went on to earn a B.A in Fine Arts from Indiana University, and in 1951 joined "the Bohemia of Greenwich Village, USA." He has since recited his poems in coffeehouses in New York, Paris and even in the middle of Saraha Desert, and has since lived in may parts of the world, from New York to Timbuktu. He resides, as a seasonal residence, in Vancouver. During the fifties he became associated with the Beat Generaion but his strongest influences are probably the surrealist André Breton, Langston Hughes and his muse Laura, whom he met in 1991 in Paris.

Allen Ginesberg and Ted Joans signing books at City Lights in San Franscisco, October 4, 1996.